T0010219

A Question of Science

Where Does Lightning Come From?

And other questions about **ELECTRICITY**

Anna Claybourne

CRABTREE
PUBLISHING COMPANY
WWW.CRABTREEBOOKS.COM

CRABTREE
PUBLISHING COMPANY
WWW.CRABTREEBOOKS.COM

Published in Canada
Crabtree Publishing
616 Welland Ave.
St. Catharines, Ontario
L2M 5V6

Published in the United States
Crabtree Publishing
347 Fifth Avenue
Suite 1402–145
New York, NY 10016

Published in 2021 by Crabtree Publishing Company

First published in 2020 by Wayland
© Hodder and Stoughton 2020

Author: Anna Claybourne

Editorial Director: Kathy Middleton

Editor: Julia Bird

Proofreader: Petrice Custance

Design and illustration: Matt Lilly

Cover design: Matt Lilly

Production coordinator and
Prepress technician: Tammy McGarr

Print coordinator: Katherine Berti

Printed in the U.S.A./082020/CG20200601

Picture credits
Alamy: Chronicle 23l; Classic Image
23r; Sergey Tolmachev 16c, 22cl;
World History Archive 18c.
Getty Images: Allan Davey 2016 1,
12t;
NASA: JPL 7tr.
Nature PL: Mark Bowler 20cl.
Shutterstock: Arcady 5b; aquapix
19tl; Thomas Barrat 29t; Batanin 7br;
Berni0004 8c; Cy bo 27t; Cobalt88
5cr; Laura Dinraths 20b; Everett
Historical 8br; FabrikaSimf 17bl;
Markus Gebauer 28b; Gdvcom 9bl;
Anton Gvozdikov 10-11; Hanohiki
14c; Daniel Heighton 6br; Humbak
19c; Jammy Photography 14cl;
Frank L Junior 8tr; Kellifamily 5tc;
Art Konovalov 25cr; Kozlik 19tr;
Kwadrat 21cr; Andrey Luzhanskiy
20cr; Sergey Marina 4b; Ekaphon
Maneechot 9bc; Mihalec 17tl;
Luciano Mortula-LGM 9br; Olga
Miltsova 29br; J Natayo 7tc; Ociacia
5c; Oksana 2010 15b; OSTILL is
Franck Camhi 29bl;
Parilov 24br; Photosite 26c; Pung
17tr; Rowo 5tr; Navee Sangvitoon
26bl; Gary Saxe 6bc; John D Sirlin
13c; Smit 25c; Ssuaphotos 6bl, 25cl;
Tristan Tan 21cl; Thanatphoto 17br;
Lee Yiu Tung 8tc; 2p2play 14tr;
Cheng Wei 20t; Alexandre Zveiger 8t.
Wikimedia Commons: Last known,
National Museum of Iraq 19b.

Library and Achives Canada Cataloguing in Publication

Title: Where does lightning come from? : and other questions
  about electricity / Anna Claybourne.
Names: Claybourne, Anna, author.
Description: Series statement: A question of science |
  Includes index.
Identifiers: Canadiana (print) 20200254243 |
  Canadiana (ebook) 20200254359 |
  ISBN 9780778778370 (softcover) |
  ISBN 9780778777076 (hardcover) |
  ISBN 9781427125392 (HTML)
Subjects: LCSH: Electricity—Juvenile literature. |
  LCSH: Electricity—Miscellanea—Juvenile literature. |
  LCGFT: Trivia and miscellanea.
Classification: LCC QC527.2 .C53 2020 | DDC j537—dc23

Library of Congress Cataloging-in-Publication Data

Names: Claybourne, Anna, author.
Title: Where does lightning come from? : and other questions
  about electricity / Anna Claybourne.
Description: New York, NY : Crabtree Publishing Company, 2021. |
  Series: A question of science | First published in 2020 by Wayland.
Identifiers: LCCN 2020023612 (print) | LCCN 2020023613 (ebook) |
  ISBN 9780778777076 (hardcover) |
  ISBN 9780778778370 (paperback) |
  ISBN 9781427125392 (ebook)
Subjects: LCSH: Electricity--Juvenile literature.
Classification: LCC QC527.2 .C538 2021 (print) |
  LCC QC527.2 (ebook) | DDC 537--dc23
LC record available at https://lccn.loc.gov/2020023612
LC ebook record available at https://lccn.loc.gov/2020023613

Contents

What is electricity?

Electricity is all around us, flowing through our houses, lighting up the streets, and making our gadgets and computers work. If we didn't have electricity, our lives would be VERY different.

WHEN WILL SOMEONE INVENT BATTERIES SO I CAN USE THIS THING?

We're all used to using things that need electricity, such as lights, TVs, toys, toothbrushes, and phones.

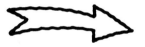

But what exactly IS it?

Electricity is a type of energy. Energy is the power to do something or make something happen. It comes in many types, or forms, such as:

Heat

Light

Sound

Movement

Energy can also be stored. For example, it is stored in the **chemicals** found in food or fuel. When your body **digests** food, or when fuel is burned, the stored energy is released.

There's a store of energy in this avocado!

Lighting was one of the first things electricity was used for.

Drones

Hairdryers

Electric world

Electricity is a super-useful form of energy because it can be used to power machines, gadgets, and tools. Since we figured out how to use energy about 200 years ago, we've invented all kinds of things that run on it.

Robots

Smartphones

How does it work?

Electricity begins with atoms, the tiny units that everything is made of.
Atoms contain even tinier parts called **electrons**, **protons**, and **neutrons**.

Atom

protons and neutrons

Electrons around the edge

Electrons and protons have **electric charges**. Electrons have a negative charge and protons have a positive charge. Atoms always try to have balance with the same number of electrons and protons. But electrons can move away from atoms.

This movement of electrons is

electricity!

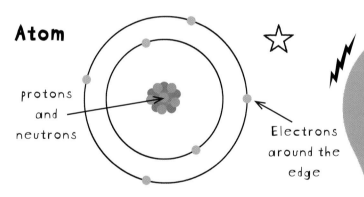

SHOCKING!

Electricity can flow through people, too, and give you an electric shock. **This can be tingly, painful, or—if it's strong enough—deadly dangerous.**

DANGER

That's why you have to be REALLY careful with electric outlets, wires, and machines.

Where does electricity come from?

An interesting thing about energy is that you can't create it from nothing. You can only turn one form of energy into another. You also can't destroy it.

For example, when you eat food...

...it turns into heat and movement energy in your body.

There are two main types of electricity—current electricity and static electricity.

For current electricity, you must start with another form of energy, such as the movement of a wind **turbine**.

The electricity flows as a current through wires to where it is needed, such as a building.

A **generator** turns movement energy into electricity by creating a flow of electrons.

Wind

When turbine blades rotate, they create movement energy.

Round and round

We make most of our electricity using turbines. Different forms of energy are used to make turbines spin.

A wind turbine is rotated by the wind.

A **hydroelectric** power station uses the flow of water through a dam to make turbines rotate.

Some power stations burn fuel, such as oil, to boil water. This produces steam, which makes turbines rotate.

Electric light

Solar panels use energy from the Sun to make electricity. They are made from a special material that makes electricity flow when sunlight hits it.

RUNNING ON SUNSHINE!

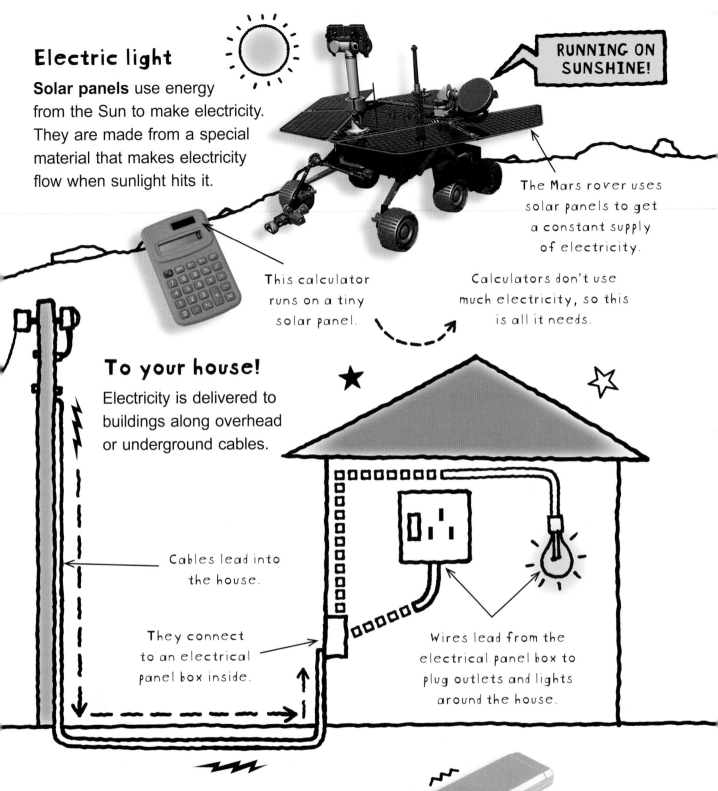

The Mars rover uses solar panels to get a constant supply of electricity.

This calculator runs on a tiny solar panel.

Calculators don't use much electricity, so this is all it needs.

To your house!

Electricity is delivered to buildings along overhead or underground cables.

Cables lead into the house.

They connect to an electrical panel box inside.

Wires lead from the electrical panel box to plug outlets and lights around the house.

Pocket supply

Electricity can also come from **batteries**. Inside a battery, a **chemical reaction** occurs to make a flow of electrons.

Batteries don't need to be plugged in, so they're useful for powering devices we carry.

How can electricity turn into light?

Since we started using electricity, life is a LOT brighter than it used to be—especially at night! Lighting is one of the main uses we have for electricity.

Christmas decorations

Lighting our homes

Streetlights

In this satellite image taken at night, you can easily spot the world's biggest cities from all the glowing lights!

A brilliant idea!

Thomas Edison is famous for inventing the lightbulb. But his version, in 1879, came after work by other inventors, such as Joseph Swan. They both used a method called **incandescence**, which is still used in some lightbulbs today.

Thomas Edison (1847–1931)

Here's how an incandescent lightbulb works.

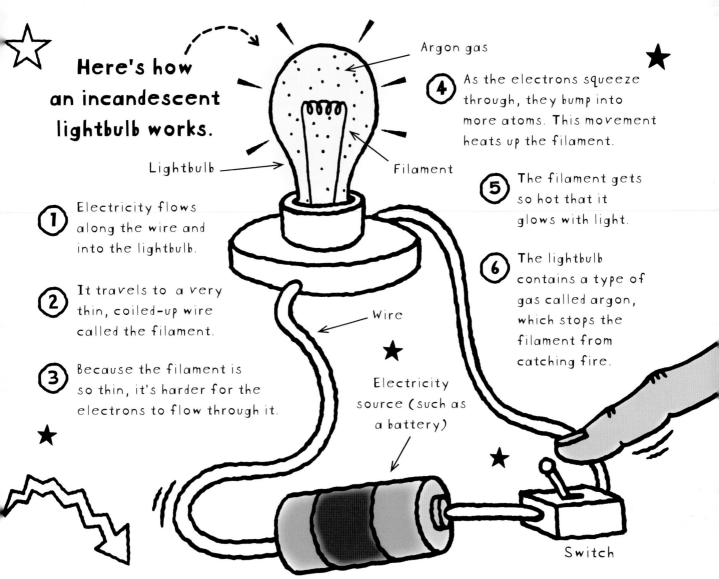

Lightbulb

Argon gas

Filament

Wire

Electricity source (such as a battery)

Switch

(1) Electricity flows along the wire and into the lightbulb.

(2) It travels to a very thin, coiled-up wire called the filament.

(3) Because the filament is so thin, it's harder for the electrons to flow through it.

(4) As the electrons squeeze through, they bump into more atoms. This movement heats up the filament.

(5) The filament gets so hot that it glows with light.

(6) The lightbulb contains a type of gas called argon, which stops the filament from catching fire.

Lots of lights!

Today we also use several other types of lightbulbs.

LED bulbs contain a material called a **semiconductor** that glows when electricity flows through it.

A halogen bulb is a type of modern incandescent bulb. It contains halogen gas, which helps the filament to last longer.

In neon and fluorescent bulbs, the electricity heats up a gas inside. This makes a special coating on the inside of the bulb glow with light.

9

OUCH!

Why do shopping carts zap you?

If you've ever been zapped by a shopping cart, you'll know it HURTS! When you touch it, there's a tiny spark or crackle, and a sharp stinging feeling.

This is a mini electric shock, caused by static electricity. It can happen with other objects, too, such as a car door, a doorknob, or even another person.

What is static electricity?

Static means "still." In current electricity, as discussed on page 6, electrons flow along a wire. With static electricity, electrons collect and build up in a material or object.

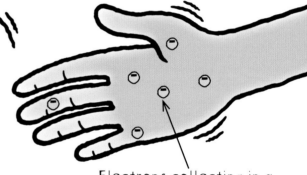

Electrons collecting in a material or object

Getting a shock

A static shock happens when electrons build up in an object and then suddenly jump from that object to another one.

Cart

Here's how it works:

When objects rub together, electrons can come off one surface and collect on another. This happens mostly with objects that electricity can't flow through easily, such as rubber and plastic (see page 16).

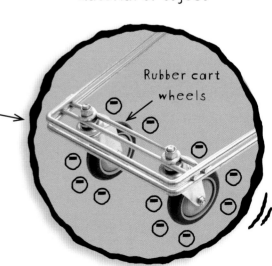

Rubber cart wheels

The electrons spread through the new object. Now the object has extra electrons, giving it a negative charge.

When a negatively charged object touches or comes close to a positively charged object they are attracted to each other, similar to a magnet. The extra electrons jump across. That's what makes the static spark or shock.

Electrons

OWW!

Electrons jumping into hand

Static balloon science!

You've probably experimented with static electricity. Have you ever blown up a balloon and rubbed it on a wool sweater?

What happened when you held the balloon against the wall?

IT STICKS!

The balloon collected extra electrons, giving it a negative charge.

The extra electrons in the balloon were attracted to the positively charged protons in the wall.

Take a charged balloon and a metal spoon into a dark room and put them close together. You might see a tiny static spark!

Where does lightning come from?

Believe it or not, lightning is pretty much the same thing as the static shock you get from a shopping cart. It's just much, MUCH bigger...

...AND MUCH more dangerous!

Lightning happens when extra electrons, or a negative charge, builds up in clouds during a thunderstorm.

Inside a cloud

Here's a large cloud in a thunderstorm.

The cloud contains lots of water droplets and ice crystals. Ice forms because it is very cold high up in the **atmosphere**.

The droplets and crystals move around and bump against each other, knocking electrons off.

The electrons collect at the bottom of the cloud.

Eventually, the extra electrons in the cloud will be attracted to protons on the ground. The flash made by the escaping electrons is lightning!

As you have probably noticed, lightning also comes with a VERY loud noise—thunder.

Where does THAT come from?

When lightning strikes, it travels along a path or channel between the cloud and the ground. The temperature inside this channel can get as hot as...

BOOOOOM!!!

54,000°F
(30,000°C)

(which is actually hotter than the surface of the Sun!)

PHEW, WHAT A SCORCHER!

This heats up the air around it very fast, making it expand and push outward suddenly.

And that makes a massive **sound wave** that we hear as a loud boom!

Don't get struck!

You do NOT want to be struck by lightning. The powerful electric shock and immense heat are often deadly. So here's how to avoid it.

If you're outside in a thunderstorm, DO stay away from high ground, tall buildings, and open spaces. The lightning will hit them first.

DON'T shelter under a tree. If it's struck, electricity can spread along the ground to you.

OW!

Don't hold metal objects, such as umbrellas or golf clubs, up in the air!

Shelter indoors if you can, but stay away from electrical appliances, metal pipes, and taps. Electricity could travel through them if the building gets struck.

Why doesn't electricity leak out of outets?

When houses first had electric outlets, some people were scared the electricity might somehow leak out of them and drip onto the floor. In fact, a few people still worry about this!

Electric outlets in the wall have holes in them so you can plug in an electric appliance to make it work.

Smartphone

Some people worry that the electricity might leak out and get wasted, making their electricity bill higher.

So can this really happen? And if not, why not?

Electrons flow around in a loop.

Battery

THAT'S A SHOCKING BILL!

Loop the loop

As you read on page 6, a current of electricity can flow along a wire. But it can only do this if the wire is in a loop, called an **electric circuit**.

If there's a gap in the loop, the electricity stops flowing. In fact, that's how a switch works. It breaks the circuit to turn a device off and connects the circuit to turn it on.

Switch

No plug, no loop

An electric outlet contains two connecting points, or terminals. When you plug in an appliance, you connect the terminals, making a circuit loop.

For example, here's a lamp:

A lamp looks like it has only one wire, but it actually contains two smaller wires.

② The wire goes through the switch and the lightbulb.

③ The wire leads back to the second terminal in the outlet.

① The wire starts at one terminal in the outlet.

When the lamp is plugged in and switched on, the circuit is complete. Electricity flows around the loop and makes the lightbulb work. If the lamp is not plugged into the outlet, there's no loop and electricity can't flow. So...

electricity can't leak out!

Then why are outlets dangerous?

If someone plays with an outlet or sticks things in the holes, they could accidentally make a circuit and get an electric shock. That's why you must always be careful around outlets.

DO NOT TOUCH!

Why are electric wires covered in plastic?

Electric appliances and their cables, plugs, and outlets can all have electricity flowing through them. Yet you can hold them and use them without getting a shock.

How does THAT work?

It's because some materials are good **conductors** of electricity, which means they let electricity flow through them, and some are not.

GOOD conductors

Metals are good conductors of electricity, especially copper. Some non-metal materials, such as salt water, are good conductors, too.

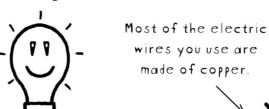

Most of the electric wires you use are made of copper.

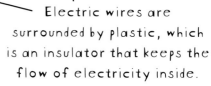

Electric wires are surrounded by plastic, which is an insulator that keeps the flow of electricity inside.

BAD conductors

Materials that don't conduct electricity well are called **insulators**. They include rubber, glass, and the plastic coating on electric wires. If wires didn't have an insulating covering like this, the electricity could flow into any other conducting objects the wires touched. That could stop the appliance from working.

Wires are dangerous to touch if they are not covered by an insulating material.

What about water?

Water is a conductor of electricity. If an appliance gets wet, it could give you a shock.

That's why you should never touch electric switches with wet hands!

ZAP!!!

Hair dryer

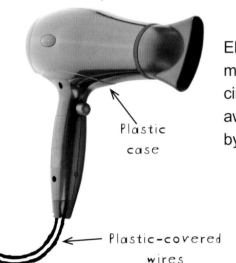

Plastic case

Plastic-covered wires

Safe to use

Electrical appliances are made so that the electric circuit is safely hidden away and protected by insulators.

In appliances that hold water, the water is kept separate from the circuit.

If an item is made of metal, such as a toaster, the outer metal parts are separate from the circuit inside. That way you won't get a shock.

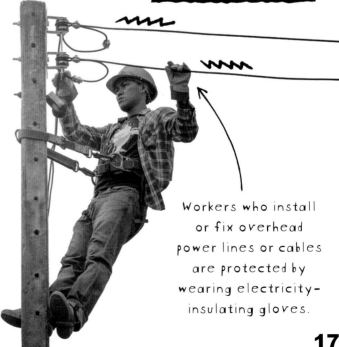

Workers who install or fix overhead power lines or cables are protected by wearing electricity-insulating gloves.

Human conductors

Our bodies conduct electricity, too. That's why electricity can flow through you and give you a shock.

Did people have electricity in ancient times?

BOOORED!

Imagine living thousands of years ago. No TV, no computer games, no dishwashers, microwaves, phones, or streetlights. None of these electrical devices existed. But was there electricity?

TAKE THAT!

Thor, the mythical god of thunder and lightning

Of course there was!

Electricity is a part of nature, so it has always existed. We didn't always understand it and use it the way we do now, but people in ancient times had some interesting ideas.

Gods and thunderbolts

Many ancient **cultures** had thunder gods, whom they believed sent down thunderbolts, or lightning strikes, when they were angry.

Sun mistake?

Some ancient Greek scientists tried to understand lightning. For example, Empedocles (495–435 B.C.E.) thought lightning must be caused by the Sun's rays getting stuck in the clouds.

Electric animals

Some animals, such as electric eels and rays, can give you an electric shock (see pages 20–21). The ancient Greeks didn't know why these fish had a strange zapping effect, but they used it as a treatment for headaches!

Electric ray

ZAPPP!

OOOH, THAT'S BETTER!

Cat fur science

Another ancient Greek named Thales (c.624–546 B.C.E.) made a strange discovery about electricity. He found that if you rubbed the gemstone amber on cat fur, the stone could pull small objects, such as seeds, toward it.

This was an early experiment with static electricity —though Thales didn't know how it worked.

Amazing fact alert!

The Greek name for amber is "elektron," which is where we get the word "electricity."

Is this a battery?

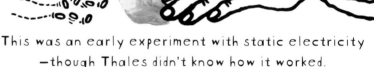

Of course, people in ancient times didn't have batteries... Or DID they???

This jar, found in ruins near Baghdad, Iraq, dates from around 1,600 years ago. Some people think it's an early battery because it has copper and iron parts with a space between them. In tests, a model of the ancient jar was filled with liquid and produced a small electric current.

Others think it was just a jar for storing scrolls that happens to be made of these materials. What do you think?

Is an electric eel really electric?

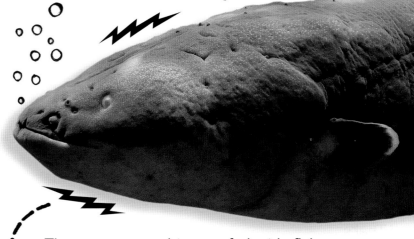

DON'T COME TOO CLOSE!

Yes, but it's not really an eel! Confused? This creature, which lives in rivers and ponds in South America, is actually a type of fish called a knifefish. But it really can give you a powerful electric shock.

There are several types of electric fish. They use electric shocks to stun or kill their **prey**, or to fight off **predators**.

Meet the E-team!

GOT MY EYE ON YOU!

Electric eel
The most powerful electric shocker

Electric ray
Over 60 **species**, including this beautiful leopard torpedo ray

Stargazer fish
Zaps predators with an electric shock from its eyes!

How do they do it?

Electric animals make electricity in a similar way to a battery, using chemicals in their bodies.

An electric eel has three large electric organs, or body parts.

The organs are made of many tiny parts. Each one works like a mini battery.

To shock something, the animal releases a chemical that makes its "batteries" work for a split second. Together, they produce a big shock—up to 600 volts! That's stronger than the electricity from an outlet in your house.

In the 1800s, explorer Alexander von Humboldt saw electric eels leap out of the Orinoco river in South America and stun two horses!

HELP!

Electric life

Electric fish might seem strange, but all animals are slightly electric. Their **nerve cells** use electricity to send signals around the body and brain.

Nerve cells in the brain

Whenever you think, move, or sense things, tiny amounts of electricity are zapping along your nerve cells, like this.

Can electricity bring something back to life?

ARE YOU SURE ABOUT THIS...

In the late 1700s and early 1800s, everyone was talking about the latest discovery—electricity. Scientists did a lot of experiments with static electricity, electric current, and lightning.

Prepare for a scary read...

Doctors used mild electric shocks as a medical treatment for problems such as insomnia, or being unable to sleep.

Galvani thought that this meant animals made electricity in their bodies to power their muscles. He called it "animal electricity." He was wrong, but the jumping leg did show how electric signals control muscles.

The jumping leg

In 1781, Italian scientist Luigi Galvani (1737–1798) was experimenting with animals and electricity, alongside his wife, Lucia. They had a frog's leg on a metal tray. When they touched it with a knife, it suddenly jumped!

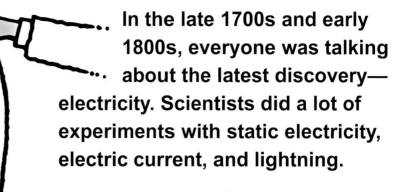

BOINNGGG!

ZAP!!

Battery power

Another scientist, Alessandro Volta (1745–1827), realized what had really happened with Galvani and the frog's leg. When the two metals in the tray and the knife both touched the wet frog leg, a chemical reaction made electricity flow—and the muscles moved.

Using this idea, Volta invented the first battery in 1799, using layers of zinc, copper, and wet cardboard.

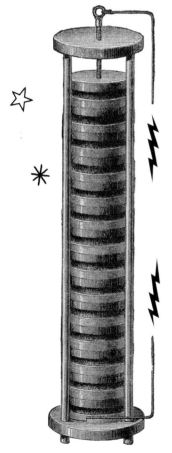

Volta's battery, the Voltaic pile

Reanimation!

Once batteries were invented, scientists could do more electricity experiments—and a gruesome new trend took off. It was called **Galvanic reanimation**, after Luigi Galvani, and it involved electrifying dead bodies to make their muscles move.

Crowds flocked to watch as scientists electrified the bodies of criminals who had been executed. The bodies would grimace, wriggle their fingers, or even sit up!

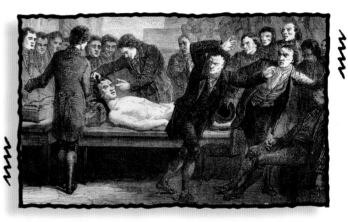

The shocked audiences thought the bodies were coming back to life—but of course, they weren't. The electricity just made their muscles move, like Galvani's frog leg.

Birth of a monster

The reanimation craze inspired Mary Shelley to write a famous novel, *Frankenstein*, in 1816. In the story, Dr Frankenstein builds a human-like monster from dead body parts, and brings them to life.

Will we run out of electricity?

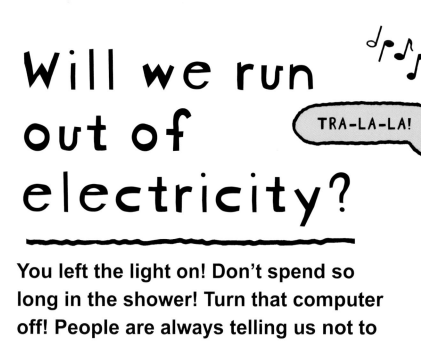

TRA-LA-LA!

Long showers use up extra electricity.

You left the light on! Don't spend so long in the shower! Turn that computer off! People are always telling us not to waste electricity.

Does that mean it's running out?

There are actually lots of reasons why you should save electricity. One is that it costs money, so wasting electricity means higher bills. There are other reasons, too—but don't panic!

Electricity is here to stay.

Ancient electricity

Fossil fuels are natural resources found in the ground, such as oil, coal, and gas. They formed long ago from the remains of living things.

Coal is dug out of the ground.

We burn fossil fuels in power stations to make electricity. But there are two BIG problems with this:

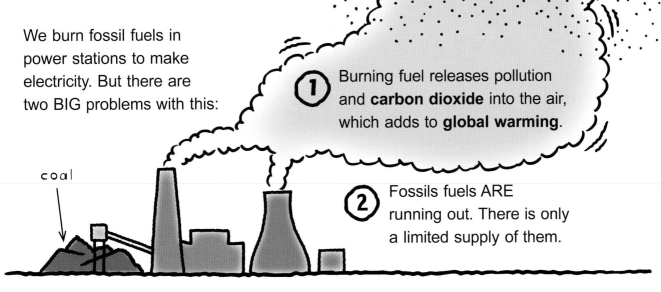

coal

1 Burning fuel releases pollution and **carbon dioxide** into the air, which adds to **global warming**.

2 Fossils fuels ARE running out. There is only a limited supply of them.

What can we do?

We still rely on fossil fuels for a lot of our electricity. But we're now switching to other methods, before it's too late! Renewables are power sources that don't get used up—such as wind, sunshine and the power of moving water. We already use several renewable electricity sources…

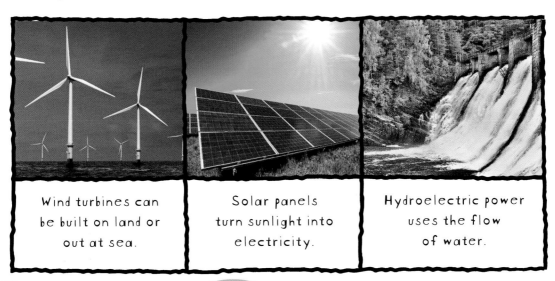

Wind turbines can be built on land or out at sea.	Solar panels turn sunlight into electricity.	Hydroelectric power uses the flow of water.

Renewables of the future

Scientists are also working on using ocean tides and waves to make electricity. The movement of water holds a lot of power and is already being used in some places. It could become a more widely used renewable source of energy in the future.

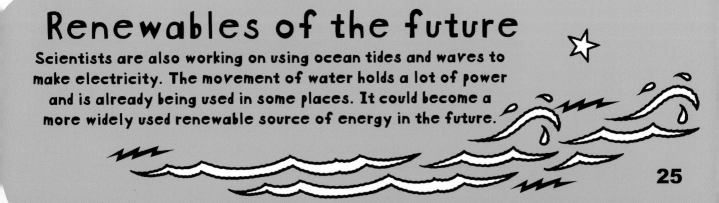

How fast can an electric car go?

In September 2016, zooming across a flat salt lake in Utah, the Venturi Buckeye Bullet 3 (VBB-3) smashed its own previous record with an incredible speed of 341 miles per hour (549 kph). It's the world's fastest electric car...

... and it looks like this!

Zooooooooom!

At the moment, most of the world's cars are not electric. They run on fossil fuels, mainly made from oil. But that's going to change as fossil fuels run out. Electric cars look like our best option.

The record-breaking
Venturi Buckeye Bullet 3

The future is electric!

We can't all drive a VBB-3, but electric cars are already on the road. Instead of a gas or diesel fuel engine, they run on an electric battery.

A Tesla Model X
electric car

The main challenge facing electric cars is that the battery needs to be charged regularly. More charging stations will need to be added along our highways.

Battery-powered buses are being used around the world too. So are electric trains that get their electricity from the rails or from an overhead cable.

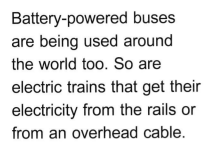

Cleaner and greener

The big advantage of electric vehicles is that they don't burn fuel and release smelly, harmful exhaust gases. With electric vehicles, the air will be cleaner and safer.

Fuel exhaust from vehicles pollutes the air, causing asthma and other health problems.

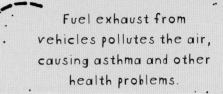

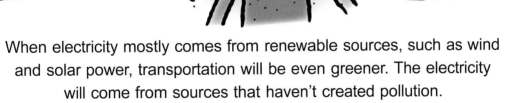

When electricity mostly comes from renewable sources, such as wind and solar power, transportation will be even greener. The electricity will come from sources that haven't created pollution.

Into the air

It's harder to make electric planes. Batteries are heavy and couldn't power a plane for very long. Scientists are working on that, too, and airlines are planning to launch electric passenger planes in the future.

Solar panels

Quick-fire questions

Why does electricity make your hair stand on end?

If you get charged up with static electricity, your whole body, including your hair, has extra electrons in it, giving it an electric charge. The charged hairs push away from each other, and the easiest way for them to get as far apart as possible is to stand away from your head. A small amount of static won't do this, but a machine called a Van der Graaff generator can give you enough charge to make your hair stand on end!

Why don't birds on a power line get an electric shock?

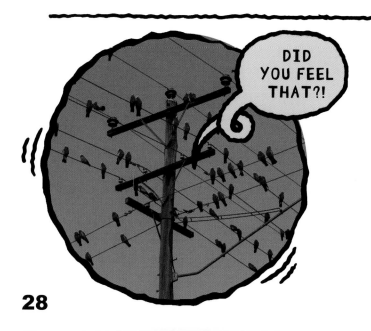

DID YOU FEEL THAT?!

Overhead electricity wires carry electricity to buildings or train lines. They can be very dangerous, but birds can sit on them without a problem. Why? The electric current keeps flowing along the wire, instead of through the bird, because that is the most direct and easy path the current can take.

What's it like to be struck by lightning?

About nine out of ten people who are struck by lightning survive. Often, they don't remember much about it, because the shock knocked them out. Some describe experiencing intense, burning pain, feeling paralyzed, and smelling a burning smell.

Is ball lightning electric?

Probably, but it's a bit of a mystery. Ball lightning is a strange, very rare occurrence that can happen during thunderstorms. Witnesses usually see a glowing, floating sphere that can pass through walls and windows. The ball eventually explodes or pops.

ZAP!!

Why are electric guitars so loud?

By itself, an electric guitar isn't very loud. If you pluck the strings, you'll just hear a faint sound. The reason electric guitars are loud is that they are usually connected to an **amplifier** and a speaker. Electric **pickups** in the guitar turn the vibrating of the strings into an electric signal. The amplifier makes this signal stronger, so that it has more energy.

Glossary

amplifier A device that increases power

atmosphere A layer of gas that surrounds Earth

atoms Tiny particles that make up all things

batteries Units that release electricity when connected to a circuit

carbon dioxide A gas found in the air and used by plants to make their food

chemical A substance that cannot be broken down into different parts

chemical reaction A process in which one or more substances are changed into others

conductors Materials that conduct, or carry electricity easily

culture The way of life of a particular group of people

current electricity The flow of electricity from one place to another, usually through a wire

digest When the body breaks down food in order to absorb nutrients

electric charge An amount of electrical energy stored in an object

electric circuit A loop of wire or another material that can conduct electricity

electric shock An injury or pain caused by electricity flowing through the body

electrons Tiny parts of atoms that can flow as an electric current through some materials

fossil fuels Materials such as coal, oil, and gas, formed underground from the bodies of animals or plants that died long ago

Galvanic reanimation Using electricity to make dead bodies or body parts move

generator A machine that converts movement energy into a flow of electricity

global warming A gradual increase in Earth's average temperature

hydroelectric power Electricity produced from the movement of flowing water

incandescence A glow of light caused by an object getting very hot

insulators Materials through which electricity does not flow well or at all

LED (light-emitting diode) A type of lightbulb that glows when electricity flows through a semiconductor

mythical Describes something or someone that comes from a story that is not true

nerve cells Cells that carry information signals around inside the brain and body

neutrons Tiny parts of atoms that have no electric charge

pickups Devices that convert sound into electrical signals

predator An animal that hunts other animals for food

prey An animal that is hunted for food

protons Tiny parts of atoms that have positive electric charges

scrolls Rolls of paper on which something is written

semiconductor A material through which some electricity can flow

solar panels Materials that convert sunlight into an electric current

species A group of closely related living things

sound wave A vibration that is produced when a sound is made and then travels through the air

static electricity A buildup of electric charge in or on an object

turbine A device that uses a movement such as the flow of wind or water to make a wheel spin

Learning More

Books

Arbuthnott, Gill. *Your Guide to Electricity and Magnetism*. Crabtree Publishing, 2017.

Christensen, Victoria. *How Conductors Work*. Lerner Publishing Group, 2017.

Graham, Ian. *From Falling Water to Electric Car*. Heinemann, 2015.

Kopp, Megan. *Maker Projects for Kids Who Love Electronics*. Crabtree Publishing, 2016.

Websites

www.sciencekids.co.nz/electricity.html
Fun electricity facts, games, experiments and videos.

www.dkfindout.com/us/science/electricity/
Clear pictures with interactive information and quizzes.

https://phet.colorado.edu/en/simulation/circuit-construction-kit-dc
Online circuit builder that lets you put parts together to make working electric circuits.

www.saveonenergy.com/how-electricity-works/
Useful explanation of electricity using animated diagrams.

www.fizzicseducation.com.au/category/150-science-experiments/electricity-experiments/
Easy and fun electricity experiments to try.

Index